burn after reading

a journaling poetry book

BY: OLENA ROSE

BURN AFTER READING: A JOURNALING POETRY BOOK COPYRIGHT © 2021 BY OLENA ROSE. ALL RIGHTS RESERVED. NO PART OF THIS BOOK MAY BE USED OR REPRODUCED IN ANY MANNER WHATSOEVER WITHOUT WRITTEN PERMISSION EXCEPT IN THE CASE OF REPRINTS IN THE CONTEXT OF REVIEWS.

ISBN: 978-1-0879-7314-2

FOR MORE INFORMATION, PLEASE VISIT:
WWW.OLENAROSE.COM

A MESSAGE FROM OLENA ROSE:

EVERYONE HAS PROFOUND MOMENTS IN LIFE — MOMENTS THAT HAVE DEFINED THEIR LIFE. WHAT ARE THE THINGS THAT HAVE HAPPENED IN YOUR LIFE, WHETHER SIGNIFICANT OR SEEMINGLY INSIGNIFICANT THAT TEND TO PLAY OVER AND OVER IN YOUR HEAD? WHAT ARE THE MOMENTS OF YOUR LIFE THAT WOULD BE 'PUT ON THE STAND' AS A REPRESENTATION OF YOUR LIFE? THESE ARE THE DEFINING MOMENTS THAT COMBINE TO MAKE US INTO THE PERSON THAT WE ARE. THIS BOOK HELPS EXPLORE ALL THAT WE ARE AND ALL THAT WE WANT TO BECOME. IT STARTS WITH YOU.

I WANT YOU TO MAKE THIS BOOK YOUR OWN: WRITE IN IT, DRAW IN IT, RIP PAGES OUT, AND STICK THINGS IN IT. ALONG THE WAY, YOU WILL BE TAKEN ON A POETIC STORYTELLING JOURNEY WITH MY NEW POETRY COLLECTION, "A GLOWING SMILE HAUNTS THEM". THERE IS POETRY ON THE FOLLOWING PAGES THAT SPEAKS FROM MY SOUL TO YOURS. WE ARE ALL IN THIS LIFE TOGETHER.

THERE IS A UNIQUE SECTION AT THE END OF THIS BOOK CALLED, 'BURN AFTER WRITING'. THESE PAGES ARE DESIGNED TO BE THERAPEUTIC AND TO HELP YOU HEAL UNRESOLVED CONFLICTS. THINK OF THESE AS LETTERS THAT HEAL BY HELPING TO STABILIZE YOUR EMOTIONS.

YOU WILL FIND PLACES TO EXPERIENCE JOY. YOU WILL FIND PLACES TO RELEASE PAIN AND HEAL. YOU WILL FIND PLACES TO EXPLORE YOUR CREATIVITY. YOU WILL FIND AN ESCAPE THROUGH JOURNALING. AT LEAST, THAT IS MY HOPE FOR YOU.

Love,
Olena

"THE MIND IS ITS OWN PLACE, AND IN ITSELF CAN MAKE A HEAVEN OF HELL, A HELL OF HEAVEN." — JOHN MILTON

Daily Checklist

Believe you can, and you will.

1
- 5 minutes of mindfulness

2
- Cleanse skin

3
- Take vitamins

4
- Eat food that fuels my body

5
- Drink water & stay hydrated

Daily Checklist

Take care of yourself.

6
- Move my body & get some fresh air

7
- Connect with friends

8
- Unplug/Unwind

9
- Journaling: Write down my thoughts and feelings

10
- Prioritize Sleep

THIS YEAR WILL BE GOOD TO ME

(tell yourself that again)

One Goal I Have	One Plan I Have

One Thing I Want	One Thing I Need

One Change to Make	One Thing to Accomplish

A New Beginning
Life begins anew.
The scars may remain,
But they are healed all the same.
A decade full of despair,
But now, a future bright as day.
It's the creases in your cheeks
That form the smile on your face.
You are happy and free,
And this energy radiates from within.
Your glowing smile haunts them,
But in you, it brings peace.

POWERFUL

SHE HAS THE POWER TO LIGHT A THOUSAND CANDLES.
HAPPINESS IS FINALLY WITHIN.
THE WORLD HAS BEEN WAITING FOR HER GLOW TO
RETURN.
AFTER A DIFFICULT ROAD,
SHE'S SEARCHING FOR THE SUN.

HER DARK SHADOW HAS LEFT,
AND THERE'S ENCHANTMENT FOLLOWING CLOSE.
LIKE MAGIC, SHE IS SET ALIGHT.
SHE SHINES BRIGHT ENOUGH FOR OTHERS NOW
TO FOLLOW HER BRIGHT LIGHT.

NOTES

What's on your mind?
It's important to release your thoughts and feelings.

GOOD THOUGHTS	BAD THOUGHTS	ANY OLD THOUGHTS

NOTES

Get it all off your chest!
It's important to release your thoughts and feelings.

GOOD THOUGHTS	BAD THOUGHTS	ANY OLD THOUGHTS

JOURNALING
This space is for you :)

JOURNALING

JOURNALING

JOURNALING

FEARLESS

Standing tall, feeling fearless.
It's a new day and a new beginning.
Exhale the past and breathe in the present.
The future is yours for the taking.
It was a long, treacherous road,
But you are no longer in pain.

Standing tall, feeling courageous -
You are strong now.
You breathe in the air around you,
And confidence seeps out of your skin.
No one is holding you back,
And no one has power over your feelings.
Keep your head tall and your spirit high.
You are fearless, and you are free!

THE ZEN OF MAKING LISTS

A CHECKLIST OF MY HOPES & DREAMS

Can't sleep? Cut out this dreamcatcher or make your own!

Today, I Learned Something New

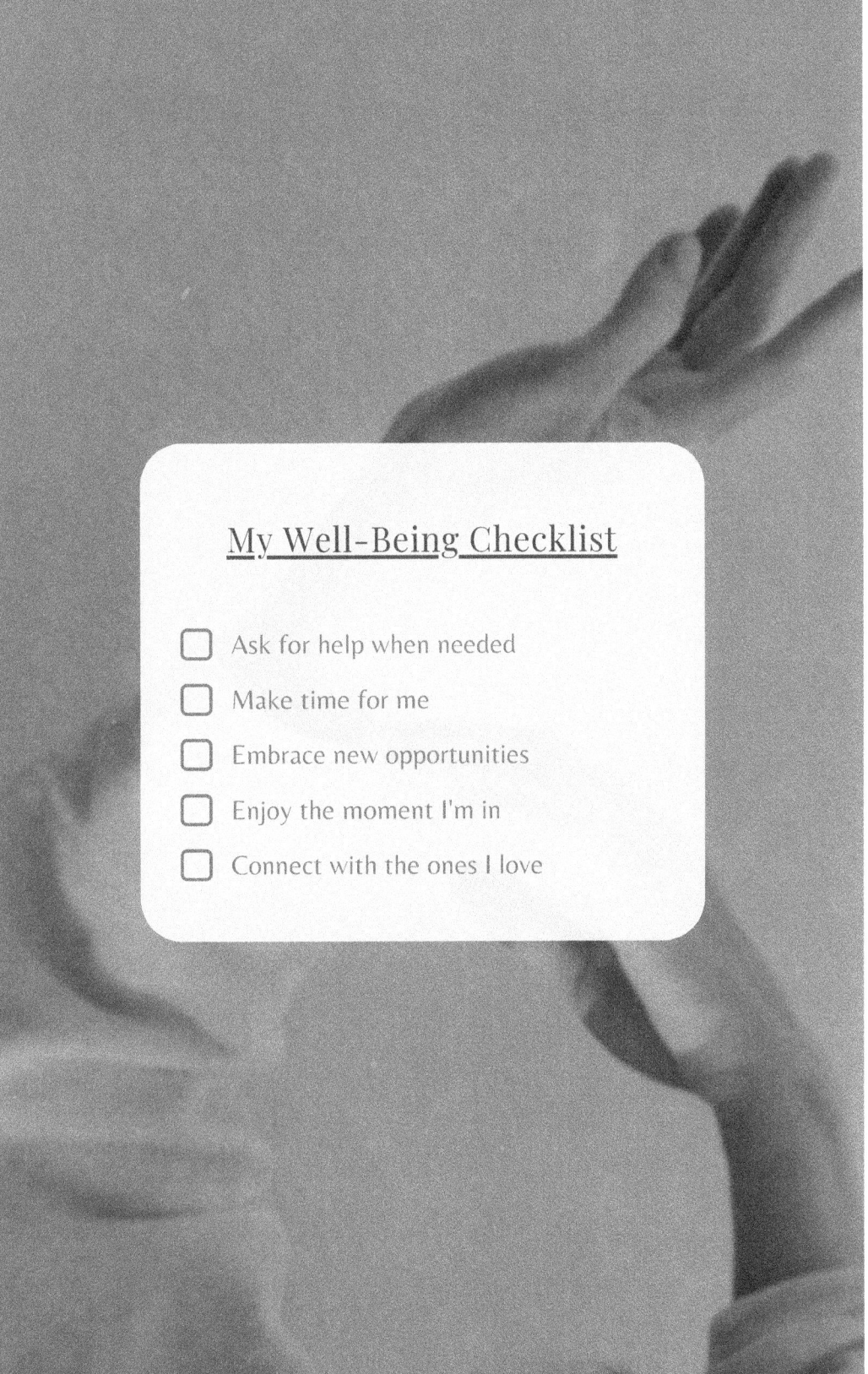

Journaling

The Drawing Board

You're Not Alone

It's a song that brings comfort.
Sometimes, that's all we need.
When the world is so dense,
But you feel like a spare part.
You are never alone in this universe.
Play the tune or sing the song.
Remind yourself that you have more,
More than you would ever know.

→

What's Going On?

Events

And everything in between...

Dates to Remember

Vision Board

IT'S SIMPLE REALLY

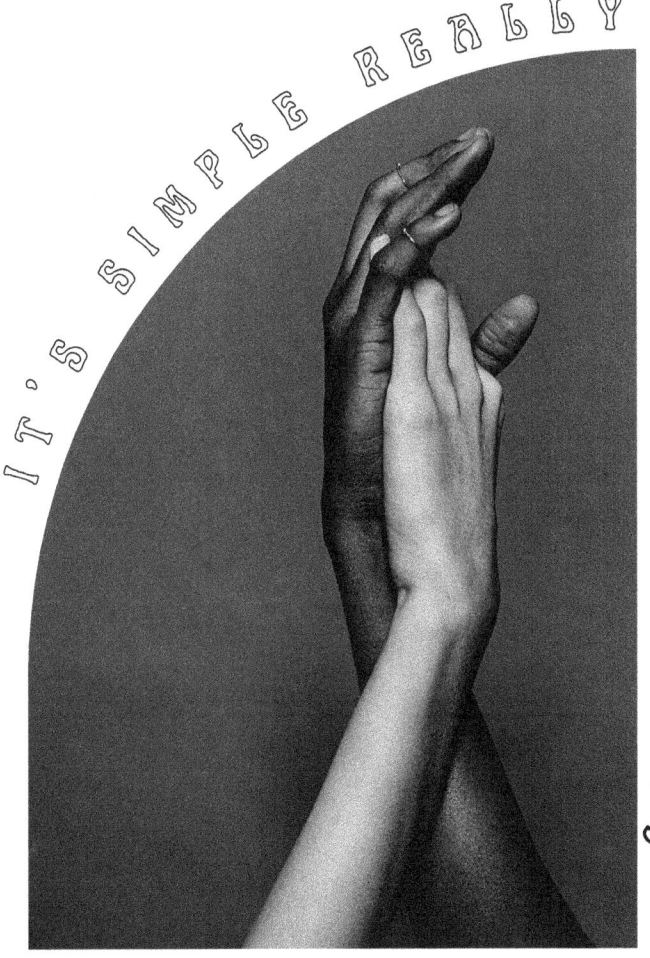

I want the world for you.
You have everything within you.
All that you see in others,
You have within yourself.
Don't doubt your beauty.
Don't doubt your strength.
Comparing yourself to others
Is taking away from your own worth.
It's simple, really.
Just focus on everything you have within,
And the envy of others will be your gain.

BE HAPPY FOR
THIS MOMENT

GRATITUDE
CHANGES
EVERYTHING

Grateful
Blessed

KILL EM WITH KINDNESS

"Kill Em with kindness."
That is what people say to do.
But, how does it make you feel?
Kindness is in your bones.
Yet, you don't want to just give it away.
Maybe kindness should only be reserved for those who deserve it most...

TACK ON SOME INSPIRATION
TAPE IT, STICK IT, DRAW IT

TACK ON SOME INSPIRATION
TAPE IT, STICK IT, DRAW IT

WE ARE, ALL OF US, ARTISTS IN OUR OWN WAY.

TACK ON SOME INSPIRATION

TAPE IT, STICK IT, DRAW IT

TACK ON SOME INSPIRATION

TAPE IT, STICK IT, DRAW IT

TACK ON SOME INSPIRATION

TAPE IT, STICK IT, DRAW IT

The Mind

The mind is all too powerful.
It makes you remember things that you wish to forget.
A simple insult or a triggering conversation comes to light,
Just when you thought you let it go.
A fight with words that you can't take back.
It plays over in your mind like 'Groundhog Day'.
It's the reliving of the past that you can't escape.
The mind takes over and makes you recreate the moments –
The moments that hurt the most.
The space reserved for bad memories is far too large.
It's like a crater in your brain that never ends.
It's filled with moments that you want to erase.
These memories will come to haunt you,
Almost like a volcano exploding within.
But once they're out, they turn to ash,
Only to return as lava at a later date…

Bucket List

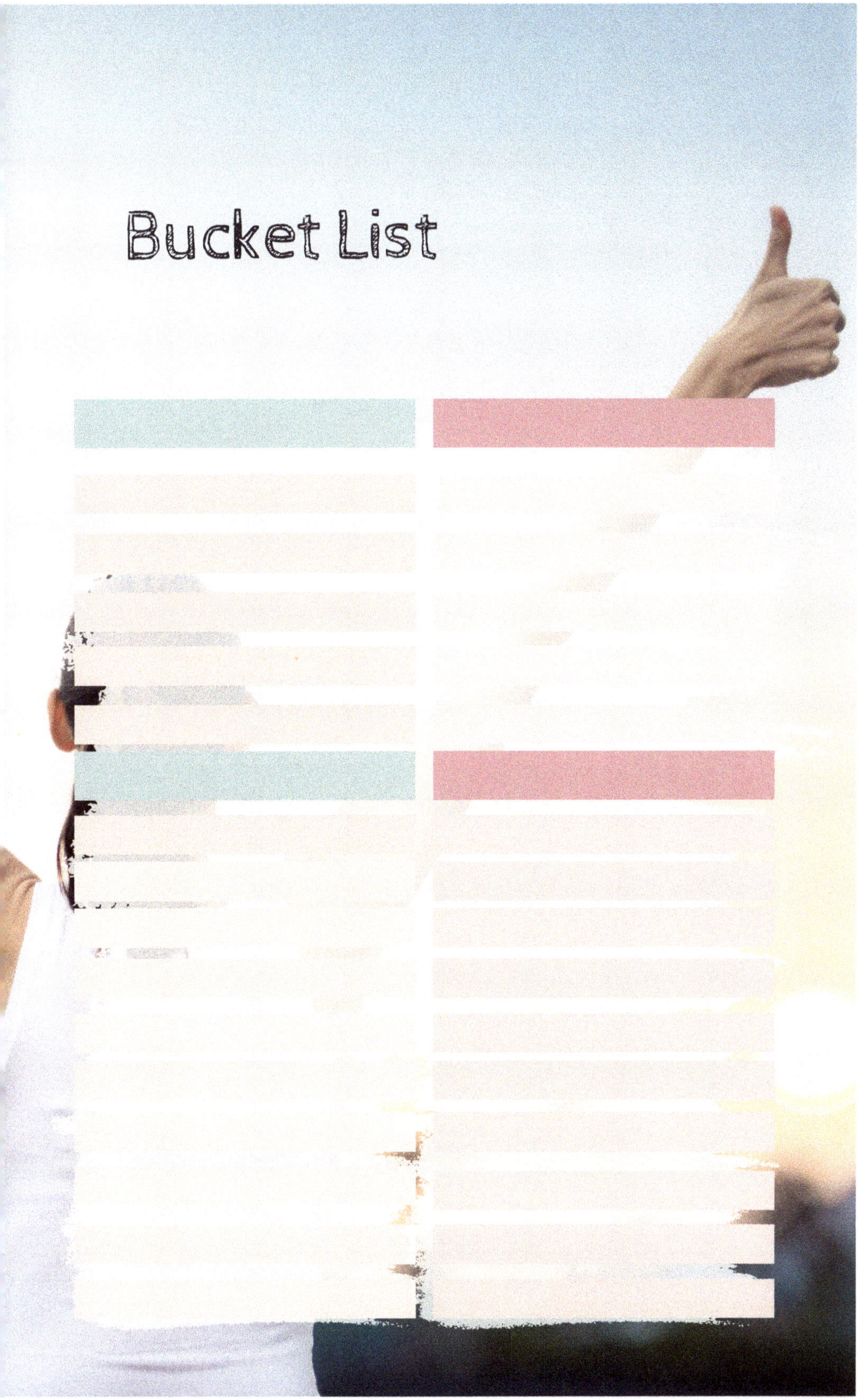

JOURNALING

Wishing Well

A wishing well and a child's innocence.
Oh dear, how I wish the world was that kind.

With just a wish on a penny and a break of the wrist,
All those little dreams unfold and travel into the universe.

If I could make them appear for you, how I would.
The little miracles that happen in life,
Maybe they are tied to those wishes.
They come out and make themselves known.

Maybe not for you, my dear.
But wishes granted, nonetheless.

Travel (realities)

- ○
- ○
- ○
- ○
- ○
- ○

DELICATE

THE SMALL OF YOUR BACK IS A DELICATE SPOT.
MAKE SURE IT'S HANDLED WITH CARE.
YOU NEED TO BE PROTECTED,
FOR YOU ARE AS DELICATE AS JASMINE ON THE VINE.
MAKE SURE YOU ARE AMONG SAFE, STRONG HANDS.
WHOEVER YOU CHOOSE TO FALL BACK ON,
MUST BE READY FOR YOU IF YOU FALL.
CHOOSE YOUR ALLIES PRECISELY,
AND YOU WILL ALWAYS FEEL TENDERNESS
ON THE CURVE OF YOUR SPINE.

THIS or THAT

MORNING PERSON	or	NIGHT OWL
READ A BOOK	or	WATCH TV
SHOWER	or	BATH
VACATION	or	R&R AT HOME
SPEND YOUR MONEY	or	SAVE YOUR MONEY
INDOORS	or	OUTDOORS
OPTIMIST	or	PESSIMIST
WRITE	or	DRAW

THEN AND NOW

When she looked back,
She saw a life that was full of grief.
When she looked around her,
She saw the beauty of the day.
When she looked ahead,
She envisioned a future full of hope.

She embraced all three,
And realized that these were the threads of life.
To embrace the grief, relish the day,
And to have hope for a new tomorrow

Open Road After *Summer*

One summer she made a mistake.
It cost her a decade of her life.
A decade crumbled behind her,
And all that remains is today.
Time doesn't really matter,
Since it's experiences that make up our fate.
The rearview mirror does nothing,
If not just magnify our mistakes.
All she can do is keep driving forward,
And embrace the open road before her.

I Can and I Will!

Write Here

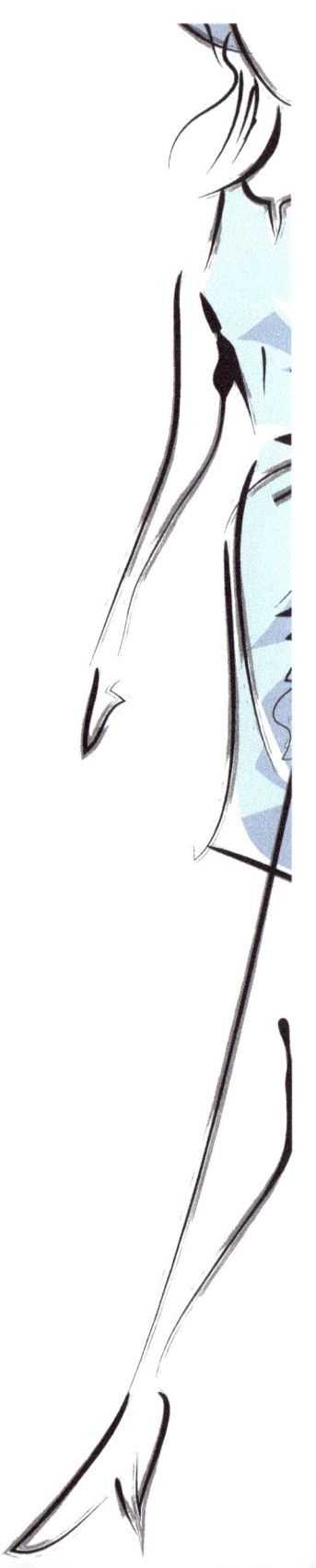

Draw Here

RoseMarie

LETTING GO OR HANGING ON,
I THINK IT'S ONE IN THE SAME.
SHE'S STILL WITH ME SOME DAYS,
AND OTHERS, NOT.
THAT IS THE ART OF MISSING SOMEONE –
AS BEAUTIFUL AND DEVASTATING AS IT IS.

This poem is dedicated to anyone you have lost that is dear to your heart.

My Sign from Above

A flicker of the light.
It's a sign from above.
Oh, how I longed for a sign.
My heart needs peace.
But, do I believe?

It happens again.
I know it's her because he showed her the way.
The light goes off,
But it always returns.
My sign from above,
And there is hope once more.

Let it Out!

Let it Out!

A Promise to Yourself

SHE PROMISED HERSELF TO START ANEW.
A NEW CHAPTER BEGINS,
BUT IT'S ALL ASKEW.
SHE CLOSES THE BOOK TIME AFTER TIME.
ALL OF HER HOPES AND DREAMS,
REPEATING IN HER HEAD LIKE RHYMES.
THIS TIME SHE WILL CHANGE.
SHE WILL HAVE THE CONFIDENCE TO SHINE.
THIS TIME WON'T BE THE SAME...

And remember,

are enough!

Fractured

Someone notices a fracture in your smile,
But you quickly look away.
It's both easy and hard
To hide the truth,
But in your heart, you know.

Sparkly from the outside looking in,
But you're tarnished through and through.
You were once a polished diamond,
And your flaws you carried proud.
But now you're stripped of your brilliance,
And it's hard to hide the grime.

Solitude

I SIT IN SOLITUDE.
WHIMSICAL THOUGHTS FLOAT THROUGH MY HEAD.
I PEER OUT THE WINDOW.
LUMINOUS BANDS ARE GLOWING IN THE SKY.
IT'S THE FIRST LIGHT OF THE DAY.
I PEER OUT THE WINDOW.
I SPOT A SILHOUETTE OF AN ANGEL,
SITTING AMONGST THE BLOOMING MAGNOLIAS.
IN THIS MOMENT I AM HOPEFUL,
AND THE WORLD SEEMS SO PROMISING.
MY GARDEN IS ENCHANTED.
IT'S SUCH A WONDEROUS VIEW.
THESE MYSTICAL FEELINGS WON'T LAST.
I WANT TO BOTTLE THEM UP FAST.
OH, THESE FANCIFUL STORIES
THAT LIVE IN MY HEAD.

HEAD IN THE CLOUDS

3am Thoughts

HEAD IN THE CLOUDS

3am Thoughts

Self Love

I am strong	I am capable	I am enough
I am unique	I am powerful	I am worthy
I am brave	I am proud of myself	I am me!

Keep reminding yourself.

___

The Tides

IN THE DEEPEST PART OF THE NIGHT,
WHEN THE WORLD IS WASHED AWAY,
YOU FALL INTO A TRANCE,
AND YOUR MIND IS DOING A DANCE.
THE MOON DICTATES THE TIDES,
JUST AS YOUR MIND DOES NOT HIDE
ALL OF THE SHELLS OF MEMORIES OF YOUR LIFE.

Write one sentence every day for a week.

Write one sentence every day for a week.

DARKNESS

LIFE CAN FEEL SO EMPTY,
LIKE A BOTTOMLESS PIT.
SO MUCH TO COME,
BUT MUCH LIKE THE PITCH BLACK OF NIGHT,
WE CANNOT SEE.
WHO KNOWS WHAT OUR FUTURE HOLDS.
WE DON'T GET TO SEE.
WHEN YOU PONDER LIFE,
THERE'S SO MUCH STILL UNSEEN.
DO NOT DESPAIR; YOUR LIFE IS NOT BARE.
THERE IS SO MUCH LEFT TO SEE.

FEARFUL

FEAR AND FRIGHT,
THEY SEEM TO EMERGE FROM WITHIN.
WHAT HAUNTS ME ON THE INSIDE?
IT MUST BE SOMETHING SO DARK AND DISTURBING
TO MAKE ME IMAGINE SUCH DEMONS.

THE FEAR CREEPS OUT OF ME LIKE A GHOST,
THEN IT ALL COMES AT ONCE.
I'M SHAKING, TREMBLING AT THE SIGHT,
BUT THERE'S NOTHING THERE...

PURE LOVE

A love so pure,
Your heart aches in awe.
A precious spectacle,
That the mind adores.

Note to self

The thing about planning is that we don't actually know what tomorrow might bring.

The thing about worrying is that it won't change anything.

The millions of meaningless fragments of time in our lives fill our heads with illusions.

We shift our focus and put too much emphasis on insignificant moments of time.

Don't incumber your head with this mindless clutter.

———————————————

GET THESE NEGATIVE THOUGHTS OUT OF MY HEAD

Write or draw the thoughts you have on your mind to release them.

GET THESE NEGATIVE THOUGHTS OUT OF MY HEAD

Write or draw the thoughts you have on your mind to release them.

GET THESE NEGATIVE THOUGHTS OUT OF MY HEAD

Write or draw the thoughts you have on your mind to release them.

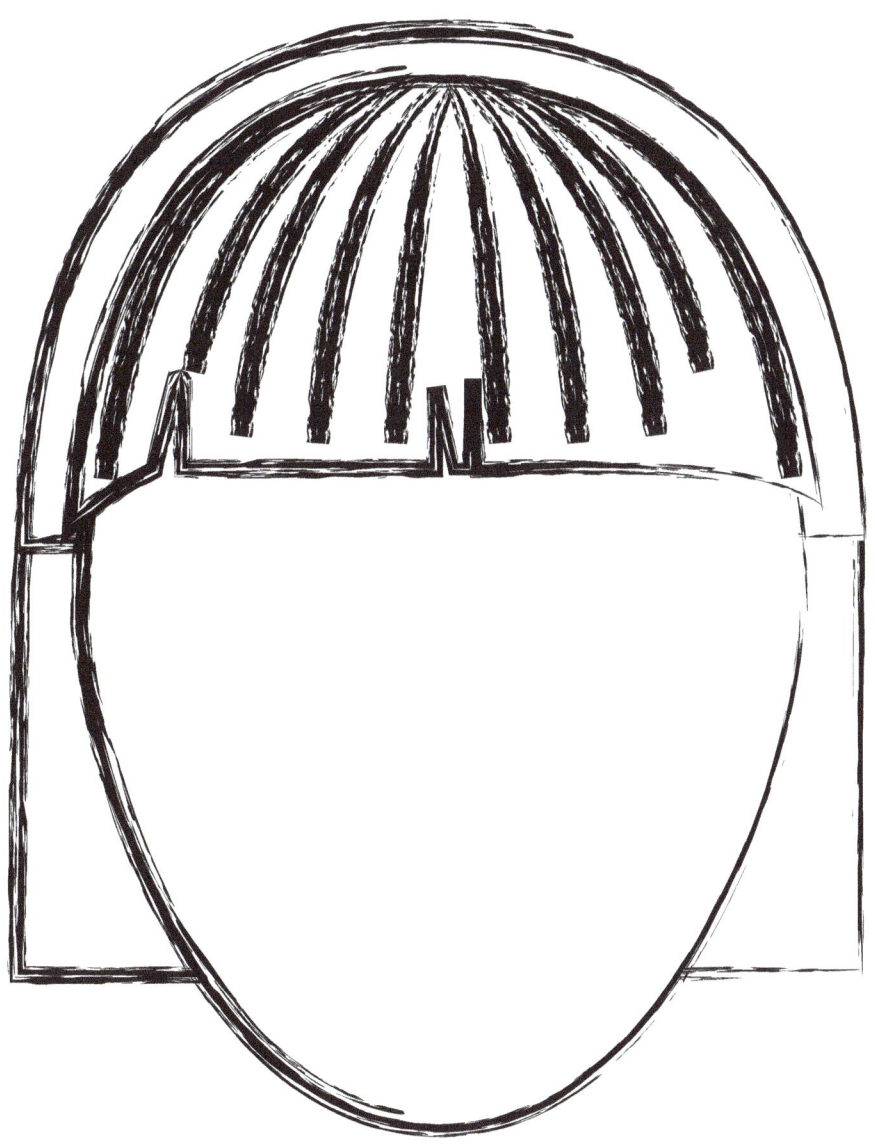

GET THESE NEGATIVE THOUGHTS OUT OF MY HEAD

Write or draw the thoughts you have on your mind to release them.

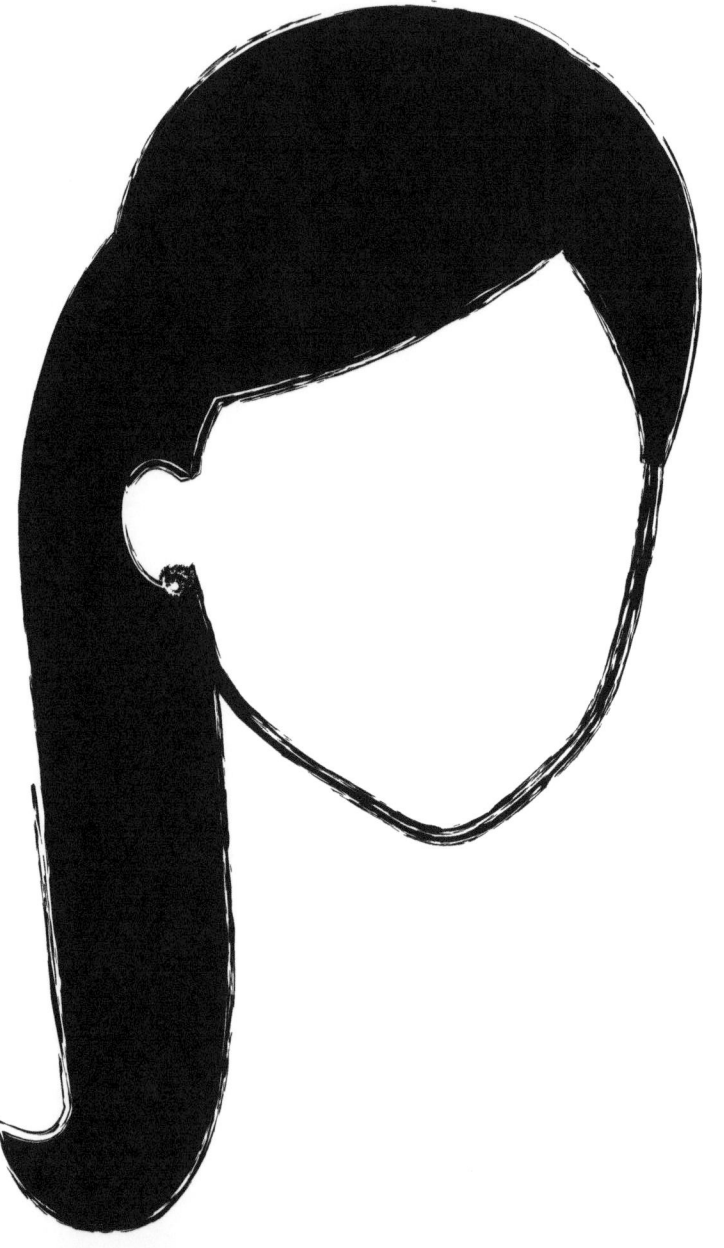

INNER CRITIC

Silence your inner critic.
She can be a nasty beast.
She will beat you up,
Unless you take away her voice.
Talk back if you have to.
Put her in her place.
She has a lot to say,
But you don't need to hear it all.
If you let her take over your mind,
You won't have peace, even for a day.

I AM

Write down all of the wonderful things that make you, you!

Burn After Writing

TEAR IT OUT AND THROW IT AWAY
(OR KEEP IT HERE TO REFLECT ON LATER)

To

Date

Subject

If you have something to say, but you're not ready to talk about it, write a letter (to yourself or to someone else) saying exactly how you feel in this moment. This is a way to release your anxiety, tension, and anger. You never even have to give it to them. Just releasing what you're feeling is sometimes all you need. Heal your pain. Let it flow - Let it go...

_____

_____

_____

_____

_____

_____

_____

_____

_____

_____

_____

_____

_____

_____

_____

Burn After Writing

TEAR IT OUT AND THROW IT AWAY
(OR KEEP IT HERE TO REFLECT ON LATER)

To

Date

Subject

If you have something to say, but you're not ready to talk about it, write a letter (to yourself or to someone else) saying exactly how you feel in this moment. This is a way to release your anxiety, tension, and anger. You never even have to give it to them. Just releasing what you're feeling is sometimes all you need. Heal your pain. Let it flow – Let it go...

_____

_____

_____

_____

_____

_____

_____

_____

_____

_____

_____

_____

Burn After Writing

TEAR IT OUT AND THROW IT AWAY
(OR KEEP IT HERE TO REFLECT ON LATER)

To

Date

Subject

If you have something to say, but you're not ready to talk about it, write a letter (to yourself or to someone else) saying exactly how you feel in this moment. This is a way to release your anxiety, tension, and anger. You never even have to give it to them. Just releasing what you're feeling is sometimes all you need. Heal your pain. Let it flow – Let it go...

_____

_____

_____

_____

_____

_____

_____

_____

_____

_____

_____

_____

_____

_____

_____

Burn After Writing

TEAR IT OUT AND THROW IT AWAY
(OR KEEP IT HERE TO REFLECT ON LATER)

To

Date

Subject

If you have something to say, but you're not ready to talk about it, write a letter (to yourself or to someone else) saying exactly how you feel in this moment. This is a way to release your anxiety, tension, and anger. You never even have to give it to them. Just releasing what you're feeling is sometimes all you need. Heal your pain. Let it flow – Let it go...

_____

_____

_____

_____

_____

_____

_____

_____

_____

_____

_____

_____

_____

_____

_____

Burn After Writing

TEAR IT OUT AND THROW IT AWAY
(OR KEEP IT HERE TO REFLECT ON LATER)

To

Date

Subject

If you have something to say, but you're not ready to talk about it, write a letter (to yourself or to someone else) saying exactly how you feel in this moment. This is a way to release your anxiety, tension, and anger. You never even have to give it to them. Just releasing what you're feeling is sometimes all you need. Heal your pain. Let it flow – Let it go...

_____

_____

_____

_____

_____

_____

_____

_____

_____

_____

_____

_____

_____

_____

TO: **DATE:**

SUBJECT:

BURN AFTER WRITING

TEAR IT OUT AND THROW IT AWAY
(OR KEEP IT HERE TO REFLECT ON LATER)

If you have something to say, but you're not ready to talk about it, write a letter (to yourself or to someone else) saying exactly how you feel in this moment. This is a way to release your anxiety, tension, and anger. You never even have to give it to them. Just releasing what you're feeling is sometimes all you need. Heal your pain. Let it flow - Let it go...

TO: **DATE:**

SUBJECT:

BURN AFTER WRITING

TEAR IT OUT AND THROW IT AWAY
(OR KEEP IT HERE TO REFLECT ON LATER)

If you have something to say, but you're not ready to talk about it, write a letter (to yourself or to someone else) saying exactly how you feel in this moment. This is a way to release your anxiety, tension, and anger. You never even have to give it to them. Just releasing what you're feeling is sometimes all you need. Heal your pain. Let it flow - Let it go...

TO: **DATE:**

SUBJECT:

BURN AFTER WRITING

TEAR IT OUT AND THROW IT AWAY
(OR KEEP IT HERE TO REFLECT ON LATER)

If you have something to say, but you're not ready to talk about it, write a letter (to yourself or to someone else) saying exactly how you feel in this moment. This is a way to release your anxiety, tension, and anger. You never even have to give it to them. Just releasing what you're feeling is sometimes all you need. Heal your pain. Let it flow - Let it go...

TO: **DATE:**

SUBJECT:

BURN AFTER WRITING

TEAR IT OUT AND THROW IT AWAY
(OR KEEP IT HERE TO REFLECT ON LATER)

If you have something to say, but you're not ready to talk about it, write a letter (to yourself or to someone else) saying exactly how you feel in this moment. This is a way to release your anxiety, tension, and anger. You never even have to give it to them. Just releasing what you're feeling is sometimes all you need. Heal your pain. Let it flow - Let it go...

TO: **DATE:**

SUBJECT:

BURN AFTER WRITING

TEAR IT OUT AND THROW IT AWAY
(OR KEEP IT HERE TO REFLECT ON LATER)

If you have something to say, but you're not ready to talk about it, write a letter (to yourself or to someone else) saying exactly how you feel in this moment. This is a way to release your anxiety, tension, and anger. You never even have to give it to them. Just releasing what you're feeling is sometimes all you need. Heal your pain. Let it flow - Let it go...

One Last Time

Write down your sorrows.
Burn them in the wind.
Let go of the illusions.
They serve no purpose now.
One last time to swim in the darkness,
Before you bask in the sunshine of tomorrow.
This is it; you are free.
Breathe in the healing air.

#ALWAYSREMEMBER

I
AM
ENOUGH.

www.ingramcontent.com/pod-product-compliance
Lightning Source LLC
Chambersburg PA
CBHW051602010526
44118CB00023B/2788